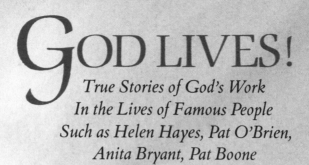

GOD LIVES!

*True Stories of God's Work
In the Lives of Famous People
Such as Helen Hayes, Pat O'Brien,
Anita Bryant, Pat Boone
And Many Others*

Edited by Shifra Stein
Illustrated by James Hamil

HALLMARK EDITIONS

GOD LIVES!

THE LORD IS CLOTHED
WITH STRENGTH

Actress Helen Hayes *tells how the 93rd Psalm calmed her spirit and gave her the strength she needed in a dark time of her life.*

SPONTANEOUS PRAYERS are usually pretty inadequate, it seems to me, when one is asking God for the impossible much of the time — or else thanking Him for making the impossible come to pass. Those prayers usually come out as "God help us" or "Thank God" or "Great God Almighty" or something of that sort. They are perfectly good prayers, of course, and do relieve one. But when the head is cleared it is pleasant, I think, to address God politely as one would any friend of whom one is seeking a favor. I have never felt satisfied with my own made-up prayers. So I very often turn to David, the Poet King, or Paul the Epistler. They are my favorites. They roar and they sing — they never wheedle or whine. They have provided me with sustenance as they have countless others through the ages....

When the news came over the radio announcing that D-Day had begun, it was as if that radio had sent me a personal message. I knew at that moment that my husband, Charles MacArthur, must be in that invasion. Only two weeks before, I had seen him off with General William Porter. Neither

5

of them would tell me what their mission was. But I knew that General Porter was Chief of Chemical Warfare, and Charlie was his special assistant. And Charlie had written from London that "lively doings" — which was a favorite phrase of his — were coming up. So, when the news came that we were sending those boats onto the beaches I suspected that he would be in one of them. Knowing my husband, I just didn't think that he could be kept out. And it was true. He and the general weren't in the first wave, they were in the second. But I knew on D-Day that they would be part of it, and I did what so many others in my home town of Nyack did — I ran to church, the Dutch Reformed Church, because I had not yet returned to my own. I wanted to say a prayer. The church was full when I got there, and I took my place in the back. There were several books in the little rack of the bench in front of me, and I picked up the Psalter — David, my ever-present friend in need. I opened the pages and began turning, searching for the 121st Psalm, which begins, "I will raise up my eyes unto the hills, from whence cometh my help." I was going to read that and get strength, because I was pretty scared. And, somehow, as I turned the pages, my eyes stopped over a new one, new that is, to me — the 93rd Psalm:

The Lord reigneth, he is clothed with majesty;
the Lord is clothed with strength, wherewith
he had girded himself: the world also is
established, that it cannot be moved.
Thy throne is established of old; thou art
from everlasting.
The floods have lifted up, O Lord, the floods
have lifted up their voice; the floods lift up
their waves.
The Lord on high is mightier than the noise
of many waters, yea, than the mighty waves
of the sea.
Thy testimonies are very sure:
holiness becometh thine house,
O Lord, for ever.

When I had finished, I knew that by some miracle I had found this one. It had been exactly what I had needed. It was the exact word, like balm to a tortured spirit. It calmed me and settled me and set me walking out of the church with my head high and new courage in my heart. I had received the strength I needed, and I knew then that I would not disgrace Charlie.

FAITH NEVER FAILS

Actor Pat O'Brien *believes that his faith is responsible for everything that he is and everything that he has.*

To THOSE WHO CLAIM that faith is purely subjective, I say with sympathy: "You've never given it a chance to act and live for you.... Ask the soldier who found faith on the battlefield — ask anyone who has come square up against it and found the vital dependable saving power of God. Miracles, some call them. The man of faith knows that guidance and help are always available when sought.

When my oldest daughter, Mavourneen, was still a child, she was stricken with a severe illness. Eloise, with the agile, loving hands of a mother, worked furiously at her bedside. Suddenly, as if touched by the hand of God, the child became well.

Eloise went all over the house looking for me. She found me praying.

"There was nothing else I could do," I told her.

"Nothing else was needed," Eloise said softly and threw her arms about me in relief.

A miracle, many people say. But I know it's just the practical and *absolutely expected answer* made possible by faith....

Faith never fails. Like an illimitable reserve fund, it is always waiting to give protection, inspiration, forgiveness, courage and spiritual joy.

I am firmly convinced that anything I am today and everything I have today I owe to my faith. It is a debt that can be repaid only by passing it on to others. I can ask no greater thrill in life than sitting in church on Sunday with my treasured mother, my beloved life-partner, Eloise, and my four youngsters, all understanding, and trying hard to serve God — all living practical faith. I wish every man and woman in the country could say with the conviction I do: "My faith is my life, my standard *for* living."

READY
TO FACE ANYTHING

In spite of threats and danger, Martin Luther King never lost his faith in God. Here, his wife, Coretta Scott King, *recalls an instance when her husband's faith was sorely tested.*

ONE NIGHT at a mass meeting, Martin found himself saying without premeditation, "If one day you find me sprawled and dead, I do not want you to retaliate with a single act of violence. I urge you to continue protesting with the same dignity and discipline you have shown so far."

On another day Martin came home feeling very weary. He said later that he had looked at me and the baby and thought, "They might be taken from me, or I from them, anytime." Then in the middle of the night the telephone rang. An angry voice said, "Listen, nigger, we've taken all we want from you. Before next week you'll be sorry you ever came to Montgomery."

It was just another of the abusive calls, but Martin felt he could take no more. He went into the kitchen and made himself a cup of coffee and began to think calmly of the position we were in and what the alternatives were. With his head in his hands, Martin bowed over the table and prayed aloud to God, saying, "Lord, I am taking a stand for what I believe is right. The people are looking to me for leadership, and if I stand before them without strength and courage, they will falter. I am at the end of my powers. I have nothing left. I've come to the point where I can't face it alone."

Martin said to me, "At that moment I experienced the presence of the Divine as I had never experienced Him before. It seemed as though I could hear the quiet assurance of an inner voice saying: 'Stand up for righteousness; stand up for truth; and God will be at your side forever.'"

Martin said that after this experience, he rose up sure of himself again, ready to face anything.

DON'T STOP NOW

As Sugar Ray Robinson *pursued his prizefighting comeback, he received some needed encouragement from God.*

"I CAN'T GET that thing," I moaned one day. By that thing, I meant my rhythm. I wasn't putting any punches together, I was flubbing on the speed bag. After the workout, Edna Mae asked me to take a walk with her.

"What's on your mind?" I asked her.

"Honey," she said, "can I say something about your boxing? About your workout?"

"Sure, you can."

"Well," she said, "it just seems to me that —"

"That what?"

"That you don't look like you used to. You look like you're trying to knock out everybody. You're so anxious to fight again, you just want to show everybody how great you once were by knocking out all your opponents. But that's not how you were great. You're not using the bag of tricks that made you great. That was your gift, the tricks were what God blessed you with, the tricks, the science, you don't use that anymore. You don't look like *the* Ray Robinson anymore."

I had stopped walking, and I was staring at her.

"You got it," I said. "You got what was wrong. All these guys around me, all these boxing guys, they don't observe that. But my wife does. My wife sees what I'm doing wrong."

The next day, I began by working on my left jab, as I had in the Salem-Crescent gym. I worked on all my punches, one by one. I checked my footwork. I checked everything. By the time I got on the train to go to Milwaukee, I felt prepared. The train arrived in Chicago early in the morning, then it swung up along Lake Michigan toward Milwaukee. Edna Mae and I were having breakfast in the dining car when the steward led a priest in a brown cassock to one of the empty seats at our table. He introduced himself as Father Jovian Lang, a Franciscan. In our conversation over breakfast, I discovered that he was going to Milwaukee for a library convention.

"May I phone you, Father?" I asked. "I'd like to talk to you about something."

He agreed, and that made me feel good. He seemed like a real guy, somebody easy to talk to. The night before the fight, he came to see me. It was as if God had sent this man to help me. I told him about my comeback, how I had lost to Tiger Jones, how I had looked bad against Johnny Lombardo. I told him that, with so many people against me, I wondered if I was doing the right thing.

"Don't stop now," Father Lang said.

"I was hoping you'd say that, Father," I said.

13

"I think God has selected you to do all this."

"But why?"

"We don't know why. It's not important to know why at this point. But if God has given you ten talents, He expects you to do ten times as much work. To sacrifice ten times as much so that you might set an example for others."

"I think I understand, Father," I said.

The night of the fight, Father Lang gave me a priest's blessing in my hotel room. I needed it. Not only to guide me in the fight but to help me through the intrigue. Shortly after I arrived in Milwaukee, I discovered that my man, Ernie Braca, also had an interest in Ted Olla, my opponent. Not only that, I had heard that Olla had been approached about letting me look good for ten rounds. Olla, to his credit, refused. The way I heard it, he said, "Hell, *I* can knock Robinson out."

Not quite. Not Ted Olla.

In the third round, I knocked *him* out. For the first time, I had that thing. I was able to put some punches together. And thanks to Father Lang, I had some confidence. It must have showed, because Joe Louis was there and when he came into the dressing room later, he shook my hand.

"BE NOT DAUNTED"

Well-known philosopher-journalist Harry Golden *discusses his mother's reaction to the term "God is Dead."*

I WAS THINKING of what my mother's reaction would be to the "God Is Dead" movement. She would have used one of the few English words she commanded. She would have said, "Foolish." Maybe "God Is Dead" was all right for some of the Protestant scholars, but how could she have cooked, fed her children, known they were safe, without God's help?

My mother never even saw a cookbook but her specialties were the best I have ever had. Yet she never took credit for her skills. Everything she did was with "God's help," even the chicken soup, or the dress she made for a neighbor's daughter.

If I told my mother God was dead she would have smiled in sympathy for such an attitude. She would have been very sad for the people who believed such a thing, and she would have repeated a favorite passage from Joshua:

> ...*be not daunted nor dismayed, for the Lord your God is with you wherever you go.*

A JOYFUL KINSHIP

Writer Anne Morrow Lindbergh *recalls a moment when she felt extreme joy in being one of God's creatures.*

OR A FULL DAY and two nights I have been alone. I lay on the beach under the stars at night alone. I made my breakfast alone. Alone I watched the gulls at the end of the pier, dip and wheel and dive for the scraps I threw them. A morning's work at my desk, and then, a late picnic lunch alone on the beach. And it seemed to me, separated from my own species, that I was nearer to others: the shy willet, nesting in the ragged tide-wash behind me; the sandpiper, running in little unfrightened steps down the shining beach rim ahead of me; the slowly flapping pelicans over my head, coasting down wind; the old gull, hunched up, grouchy, surveying the horizon. I felt a kind of impersonal kinship with them and a joy in that kinship. Beauty of earth and sea and air meant more to me. I was in harmony with it, melted into the universe, lost in it, as one is lost in a canticle of praise, swelling from an unknown crowd in a cathedral. "Praise ye the Lord, all ye fishes of the sea — all ye birds of the air — all ye children of men — Praise ye the Lord!"

GOD'S OPEN DOOR

Author A. J. Cronin *was a bitter and disappointed man — until God's plan for his life was revealed.*

THIRTY YEARS AGO, when I was a doctor in London, on the point of moving to a specialist's practice in Harley Street, my health broke down. I was told that I must take a year's rest and that, even so, I might never again be fit to stand the wear and tear of medical life.

What a blow! I liked my work. From the humblest beginnings in a small Welsh mining practice, I had slaved to achieve this objective. And now, on the threshold of success, the door was slammed in my face. My state of mind was such that I could not help voicing bitterness and resentment to my friends.

One of these was an old Irish nun, the Reverend Mother of the Bon Secours, a small order of nursing sisters who occupied a house quite near mine in Westbourne Grove, and who frequently looked after my patients. She heard my outburst in silence, then said:

"You know, Doctor, we have a saying in Ireland, that if God shuts one door, He opens another."

I did not give her remark a second thought and soon after left for my place of exile, a remote district in the West Highlands. Here time hung heavy upon my hands. Suddenly, out of the blue, I

18

had an impulse to write. I began a novel, "Hatter's Castle," and I finished it, packed it up, and sent it to a publisher — who accepted it! Out of all reason, a door had opened. A new career lay before me.

WHAT GOD IS LIKE

I did not know what God is like
Until a friendly word
Came to me in an hour of need —
And it was God I heard.

I did not know what God is like
Until I heard love's feet
On errands of God's mercy
Go up and down life's street.

I did not know what God is like
Until I felt a hand
Clasp mine and lift me when alone
I had no strength to stand.

I think I know what God is like,
For I have seen the face
Of God's son looking at me
From all the human race.

James Dillet Freeman

"VICTORY OVER FEAR"

Dr. Norman Vincent Peale *found God while vacationing with his wife, Ruth, at an English country inn.*

*A*S WE SAT TOGETHER on that bench that afternoon I again started the dismal recital of my fears. I told Ruth for the thousandth time how discouraging everything was, how tough it was going to be back home. I listed my problems, all of them seemingly so formidable. I expressed my complete assurance of failure.

Then it happened, one of the top experiences of my life, the beginning of a thrilling adventure in personal change and unexpected but notable victory over fear. My wife Ruth is a gentle, kindly soul but when she gets aroused and becomes firm, brother, she is really firm. Turning to me she said, "Please stop this negative talk. I've heard enough of it. What are you — a phony? You *teach* faith — haven't you any yourself? Or are you only a lot of meaningless words? Doesn't God and Jesus Christ mean anything to you?

"God has given you great potential ability and has called you to unprecedented opportunity for service. You are equal to it if only you will forget yourself. All you think of is yourself — you are involved, tied up, dominated by yourself. And so you walk in gloom and fear until life is hardly worth it. I am so very sorry for you."

Then she took my hand in her smaller hand. How soft I always thought it was on moonlight walks, but it wasn't soft now. It had a powerful grip on mine and she said firmly, "You are going to sit right here with me on this bench until you surrender yourself, and your fears, to Jesus Christ."

Then I, who was her pastor, who had been educated in theology, meekly asked, "But how does one surrender? What do I do and say? How can I let go?"

I can hear her yet speaking out of the native wisdom of the truest heart I've ever known. She said simply, "Say dear Lord I now give myself, my life, my mind, my body, my soul to You. I give You all my fears. If You want me to fail I am willing to accept failure. Whatever You do with me is all right with me. Take all of me. I surrender everything to You."

Haltingly I repeated the words after Ruth and in that moment I meant what I was saying, really meant it. That prayer went down deeply into my mind, and came up with the truth, with absolute truth. Suddenly all tension and unhappiness went out of me. I could literally feel it go like a stretched rubber band returning to normal. A sense of happiness — joy is a better word — such as I had never felt before in my life surged through my whole being. I had never felt anything like it in my entire experience.

The relief I felt was so intense, so overwhelming as actually to be painful, like a deep wound emptying itself of infection; but that sensation soon gave way to one of indescribable relief. If I never have it again I had it once: a sense of God's healing Presence so powerful and unmistakable, so real, that I knew for a certainty that He is and does touch our weak human lives with His amazing grace and power.

GOD BLESSED OUR MARRIAGE

As the day of her wedding approached, entertainer Anita Bryant *became aware of a potential problem in the marriage.*

TIME MOVED CLOSER to June 25, the date Bob and I had set for our wedding. We both were so busy, so separated from one another, and still there remained one vitally important issue for us to settle.

The fact was: Bob and I had not talked sufficiently about our religious faith. He knew about mine, of course, and I knew he understood and approved of the place I reserve for God in my life.

But what about Bob? Like many other Swedes, he had been reared in the Lutheran denomination, which I greatly respect. But Bob had not been saved; he frankly admitted to being just a nominal

23

Christian, and even looked somewhat puzzled when I tried to explain what I meant by being saved through Christ.

Had God not stepped in and taken over, this could have been a terribly dangerous place in our relationship. As our wedding approached, I became more and more serious. Bob, always sensitive to what is happening inside me, could see that I was in the process of turning everything about our forthcoming life over to the Lord, for His blessing and protection.

Bob sensed the solemnity of this thing. The night before our wedding, we went to see our minister and then we talked with Gloria Roe, my close friend in Christ....

I'll never forget the closeness among us as we knelt and asked God to bless our marriage. In a true sense, that commitment felt as deep and important as the actual ceremony to come.

As we talked — as Gloria gently drew Bob out about his Christian beliefs — something wonderful happened. The Spirit of God descended upon us. Bob felt led to confess Jesus Christ as his Lord and Saviour.

This came as the holiest, most amazing gift to our impending marriage. The radiance of that moment lingered through those final hours before our wedding and started our life together in perfect joy.

GOD'S HELP

"Sitting around waiting for a call from heaven" is not the way to receive God's help, according to Margaret Mead, *author and anthropologist.*

"GET THE DISTAFF READY, and God will send the flax." These were words my grandmother used to say. She said them, not as a promise or an admonition, but as a simple statement of fact about the way the world worked. I used to spend a lot of time thinking what it meant. The distaff was a man-made tool, shaped for a special purpose, that of making thread. It was intended for no other use. So the proverb, I decided, meant that we must "meet God halfway," doing our best to help ourselves. But also, it meant we have to be specifically ready for opportunity, not just virtuously sitting around waiting for a call from heaven. We have to know exactly what we mean to do, and be fully prepared to do it — with God's help.

It's good to make plans, to dream of a distant goal, but only if the dreaming is accompanied by realistic effort on our part. When I was a child, this idea seemed a simple way of saying that life was to be trusted, like the motto that hung in the office of a country doctor whom I loved: "All things work together for good to them that love God." Later it came to mean something else to me

25

too, something very special about the strength of American character, which has this very combination of trust and enterprising effort.

We cannot bind the future by making rigid plans and stubbornly sticking to them. But we can instead get the distaff ready for the thread which is not yet spun and for which there is as yet no flax.

SOMETHING OF GOD

I hear and behold God in every object, yet understand God not in the least,
Nor do I understand who there can be more wonderful than myself.
Why should I wish to see God better than this day?
I see something of God each hour of the twenty-four, and each moment then,
In the faces of men and women I see God, and in my own face in the glass,
I find letters from God dropped in the street, and every one is signed by God's name,
And I leave them where they are, for I know that wheresoe'er I go
Others will punctually come forever and ever.

Walt Whitman

ON BECOMING
A GRANDMOTHER

Noted author Marjorie Holmes *offers a beautiful prayer for a very special occasion.*

SO NOW I'M A GRANDMOTHER, God, and I am truly grateful.

Awe fills me. A sense of excited achievement. I want to laugh, I want to sing, I want to go down on my knees.

I also want to cry. For sheer delight, yes, and for tenderness. But also just a little bit for me.

A part of me isn't quite ready to be a grandmother, God. A vain, silly, private-life-hugging part of me.

The very word sounds so final. Old. Smacking of rocking chairs and easy slippers. Of being shooed into a corner to bake the cookies, knit the mittens or merely dandle grandchildren on my lap.

And that isn't true anymore. Not for most women — and oh, God, don't let it be for me.

However I adore this grandchild and will love those to come, don't let me become too absorbed in it. Let me keep my own work, my own interests, my own identity.

(Come to think of it, everybody will be better off if I just keep on being me.)

And now that I've confessed my reservations, let me accept this new phase of my life proudly.

Grandmother...I will grasp and savor the true beauty of that word — its grandeur and its glory. To be a grand — mother. What a compliment. May I live up to it.

Thank you, God, for revealing the wonder of becoming a grandmother to me.

I HAVE HEARD
THE SONG

I have not seen the robin but I know he is there because I heard him singing through my window from the tree-top outside.

I have not seen God. But I have looked at my child's eyes, and have been overwhelmed by the miracle of unfolding life.

I have watched the trees bedeck themselves with new garbs of green in the spring, and have been stirred by the miracle of continual rebirth.

I have looked at the stars, and have been overcome by the miracle of the grandeur and majesty of the universe.

I know that God exists, because I have heard the song of His presence from all the tree-tops of creation.

Ben Zion Bokser

GOD HAS THIS
UNDER CONTROL

Entertainer Pat Boone *and his wife, Shirley, were in serious financial difficulty. He and a partner had purchased the Oakland Oaks basketball team, an investment which had not been successful for them. Facing total bankruptcy, Pat turned the problem over to God.*

I BEGAN TO SAY that God was solving it! My friends would look at me as though I was out of my mind. Meanwhile, my own financial advisors…were doing their best to come up with an answer. They tried to interest large companies in buying the Oaks. They attempted to persuade a group of wealthy people to take over the franchise. They tried to arrange long-term financing at banks, until we could make a turn-around in Oakland. They would get close to one of these answers and then strike out, time after time.

My partner Ken went all over the country, even to Switzerland, vainly trying to come up with a solution. Yet the more we struck out and the *worse the problem became,* the more Shirley and I relaxed. We knew the solution wouldn't come until God's own time, and however He solved it, it would be perfect — and He would get the glory for the way in which He worked it out….

We'd smile and say, "Don't worry. We know God has this under control."

But it was hard to smile the Monday that the bank sent me a letter itemizing various loans and asking me immediately to send a check for $1,300,-000!...The letter read like the one you might get from the telephone company. "If you have already sent your check, just ignore this notice."...

...My attorneys called for a conference. They asked that Shirley be present because they wanted her to have the picture too.

"Here's what is going to happen," they said. "The Oakland Oaks are going to go bankrupt immediately. Then the creditors will come against your partner and quickly bankrupt him. Next they will come against you. We believe we have a fighting chance to have them attach everything you've got and wait, rather than throw you into bankruptcy. Everything possible will be sold, and then you'll be able to work off the indebtedness over the next five or ten years. We think that's the best we can hope for, and, Pat, we're very sorry."

"Fellas, you've done your best," I said. "We appreciate it. Now that we all give up — watch! God is going to solve this."

They looked up at us as though we were two obsessed, crazy people. They said, "But Pat, you don't understand. It's out of our hands. It's now in the hands of the bank."

We said, "You fellas don't understand. *The bank*

is in the hands of God."

They left shaking their heads.

Two days later the news was on TV and in the newspapers. A man by the name of Earl Forman from Washington, D.C., went to the bank in San Francisco and bought the Oakland Oaks, for close to $2,000,000! I've never met the man, but when I do, I think I'll hug him. As far as I know, he doesn't realize he was part of a fantastic miracle of God, in answer to prayer. But then, neither did Pharoah in Moses' day! In about a week the negotiations were completed and the Oaks moved to Washington where they were renamed the Washington Caps.

Isn't God wonderful?

ON HIGHER GROUND

Dale Evans Rogers *writes of a troubled time in her life which led her to experience a supreme joy and happiness.*

WHEN A MAN is so burdened with a heavy load that he cannot rise up and walk, there is, plainly, only one thing to be done. The load must be removed.

I look at people all around me and wonder how many of them know what really is the matter with them—how many understand the load of sin and guilt they have been carrying for years that has kept them down, spiritually. They are filled with doubt, suspicion, envy, fear and futility; they find joy in nothing, and they wonder what is wrong!

I could tell them what is wrong. I, personally, carried such a load of sin and guilt for twenty-five years. I was a pretty sorry case, spiritually, when my son Tom asked me in church one night if all was well with my soul. I can vividly remember drawing myself up in indignant, shocked "surprise" that he would ask me such a question, and answering, "Why of course all is well with my soul. I'm all right. I accepted Christ when I was ten years old!" That should have settled it.

It settled nothing. Inside, my defenses were crumbling, and all my desperate efforts and words couldn't hide that. I saw tears in my son's eyes, and I knew that he was looking with the eyes of Christian understanding and compassion right down into my darkened soul.

I very nearly broke into tears, there in the church, but somehow I fought them back. At home, later, the dam broke, and in a flood of tears I saw that Christ had reached out through my beloved boy and redeemed a lost sheep. I called Tom and told him he was right, and that I would go to church the following Sunday, make my peace with Christ, take a public stand and unite with the church. I did just that. Thus was the burden slipped from my back; thus was I enabled to get up and walk again in a world so beautiful and full of joy that I could scarcely believe it!

In an instant, as I stood there in my bedroom facing myself in horror and throwing myself on His mercy, *everything* was changed; the world and my life were different from that moment on. The relief, the joy and the knowledge that He had set my feet on "higher ground" was the greatest experience of my whole life.

There has never been any question in my mind since that Sunday when I handed Him my soul. Oh, yes, there have been temptations to sin, worry, anxiety, shattered personal dreams, loss of loved ones — but all this was my weakness, not His. He has remained the strong high rock in the storm and stress, and never have I failed to find comfort and wisdom and strength in that Rock!

> *"Lo, I am with you always, even unto the end of the world." Lord, my whole life rests on that, now.*

THE BLOOD RAN
TO MY HEAD, LORD,
AND I ALMOST FLIPPED

Malcolm Boyd is an Episcopalian priest whose prayers deal with everyday situations and are written in current language. Here, he writes about anger.

I WAS MAD and couldn't think clearly. Thanks for cooling me down.

If I'd been on my own, I would have done something bad to somebody whom you love just as much as me. I was very vulnerable, Jesus, and he didn't realize he'd hit me in a spot so soft I should put up a neon sign over it that flashes "danger" 24 hours a day.

He hit, and I screamed inside, which is the worst kind of screaming. Then the heat flashed, and I couldn't make sense and just wanted revenge. I wanted to hurt him, Jesus.

When I simmered down, I was still sitting there, and he was still sitting there. I knew I was okay, that I hadn't done anything that would really louse everybody up.

Thank you, Lord, for being there with me and cooling me down. Thanks for taking hold of me.

FAITH BEGINS
AT HOME

Comedian and former Sunday school teacher Dick
Van Dyke *believes that children can absorb the religious faith of a warm and loving family.*

THE BEST PLACE for a child to learn religious
faith is at home, in the bosom of a family
where faith is lived and practiced. Faith isn't
something that is taught; it's something kids absorb through example in a warm and loving family
where the people tend to address themselves to
God aloud at the dinner table, or in nightly prayers.
With religion a part of daily life, a child gradually
develops an understanding of faith...a feeling for
what it really is.

We've always said grace together in the Van
Dyke family, and when the children were little,
they always said their nightly prayers with us. We
encouraged them to pray any time at all, and anywhere they happened to be.

When we moved to the Arizona desert, my
14-year-old daughter, Stacy, made a statement
that I've never forgotten. She said, "When I go
walking on the desert, I realize I don't have to go
making up words...I don't have to talk to pray...
there's just an awareness of the Presence. I acknowledge the Spirit of God right where I am.
That's praying. I know I've established a com-

munication between myself and my Maker without having to talk."

That's just how I feel, too. Any moment in your waking hours when you are aware is a prayer. The Lord knoweth before you ask, as the scriptures say, so you really don't have to say your thoughts aloud.

MY SPIRITUAL ADVENTURE

It was a time of soul-searching for Catherine Marshall *as she lay ill with tuberculosis. Here, she recalls how God helped her regain her health and her faith.*

PRIVATELY, with tears eloquent of the reality of what I was doing, I lay in bed and prayed, "Lord, I've done everything I've known how to do, and it hasn't been good enough. I'm desperately weary of the struggle of trying to persuade You to give me what I want. I'm beaten, whipped, through. If You want me to be an invalid for the rest of my life, all right. Here I am. Do anything You like with me and my life."…

In the early hours of the next morning something awakened me. The luminous hands of the clock on my nightstand said that it was 3 A.M. The room was in darkness, that total darkness known only to the country, where there are no street lights….

38

"Suppose," I mused, "I could talk to Jesus, as those people did, and ask Him to cure me, I wonder what He would tell *me* to do?"...

Suddenly, with new resolution, I almost sat up in bed. I had no sooner breathed the question, "Lord, what *would* You ask me to do?" when it happened. Past all credible belief, suddenly, unaccountably, Christ was there, in Person, standing by the right side of my bed. I could see nothing but that deep, velvety blackness, but the bedroom was filled with an intensity of power, as if the Dynamo of the Universe were there. Every nerve in my body tingled with it, as with a shock of electricity. I knew that Jesus was smiling at me tenderly, lovingly, whimsically — a trifle amused at my too-intense seriousness about myself.

"Go," He said, in direct reply to my question, "Go, and tell your mother. That's easy enough, isn't it?"

I faltered. What would mother think? It's the middle of the night. She would think I had suddenly gone crazy.

Christ said nothing more. He had told me what to do. It was clear to me that I could take it or leave it, but that if I did not obey, the chance might be gone forever. In a flash, I understood the real freedom of choice God always allows His creatures. I also understood, on the other hand, why Thomas had knelt in adoration at this One's feet crying, "My Lord, and my God." There was supreme kingliness here, as well as a human personality more vivid, more compelling than that of anyone I had ever met. It would be difficult *not* to obey Him.

"I'll do it, if it kills me," I said, climbing out of bed, sensing even as I did so, the ludicrousness of my own words. Somehow, I knew that Christ's eyes flashed humor as He stood quietly aside to let me pass.

I groped my way into the dark hall to the bedroom at the other end, and spoke softly to Mother and Dad. Naturally they were startled. Mother sat bolt upright in bed. "What — what on earth has happened?"

"It's all right. Don't be alarmed," I reassured them. "I just want to tell you that I'll be all right now. It seemed important to tell you tonight."

"What has happened?" Dad repeated.

"I'm sorry to have wakened you. I'll tell you all about it in the morning. I promise. It's too long a story for tonight. Everything's all right."

When I returned to the bedroom, that vivid Presence was gone. I found myself more excited than I have ever been before or since, and more wide awake. It was not until the first streaks of dawn appeared in the eastern sky that I slept again.

As it turned out, the healing of my lungs came slowly, no doubt because my faith grew slowly.

The next X rays showed, for the first time, definite progress. Thereafter, there was steady, solid healing, never with the least retrogression, until finally the doctors pronounced me completely well.

NOTHING SHORT OF A MIRACLE

Singer Kate Smith *knew that God was never too busy to listen to prayer.*

I WAS SITTING CALMLY in a beauty parlor having my hair set when it happened. A spark flew out of a defective hand cooler and ignited the cotton wadding around my head.

In an instant the cotton flared up — my hair was on fire!

The frantic operator flailed at the flames, but before he could put out the fire, my eyebrows, eyelids, face, and arms were badly burned. For weeks I lay in bed with my head completely bandaged. Around me I kept hearing whispered consultations. The doctor said something about my eyes.

They were gravely concerned about my sight. I was worried too, yet I had practically no fear. A calm faith took over and steadied me more than could have any professional assurance. I believe deeply in prayer, and in this case it was simply a matter of turning everything over to God.

When the time came for the bandages to be removed, my lashes had grown back, there was not even a blemish on my face, and my sight was intact. To the doctors, my recovery was nothing short of a miracle. If it was a miracle, it was because of my prayers and faith.

"Don't ever be afraid to go to God," I was once told. "He's One who will never tell you to come back some other time when He's not so busy."

AND THEN IT HAPPENED!

As a young girl, entertainer Ethel Waters *found the peace she'd been seeking inside a neighborhood church.*

M Y SEARCH FOR GOD and my finding of Him were to begin in one of those Protestant churches where they were having a children's revival. It was there that I came truly to know and to reverence Christ, the Redeemer.

All my girl friends in the neighborhood were going to this children's revival. I went religiously, every day. When the preacher, the Reverend R. J. Williams, called those who wished to repent and be saved, all my gang would go up there to the mourners' bench and kneel down — but not for long. They would pop up quick as hot cakes and as though they had brand-new souls. But we stout hearts in the back knew they hadn't been cleansed of sin but were just trying to attract attention.

"Come up and shake my hand," the Reverend R. J. Williams would say in his booming voice. "Don't you want to be little soldiers of the Lord?"

Two or three times I did go up to shake his hand. Then I'd return to my seat. I wasn't sure I wanted to be saved. "What can I ask God?" I kept thinking. "What have I got to say to Him?"

One night there were only three of us youngsters still left unsaved in the whole congregation. All the rest had gone to the mourners' bench and been redeemed.

"Come!" cried the Reverend Williams, an inspired and fiery preacher. "Get down on your knees and pray to our Lord!"

So I thought, "I will get down on my knees and pray just to see what happens." I prayed, "O Lord! I don't know what to ask of You!"

…Every night I was on my knees — and nothing happened. I didn't feel purged of sin or close to the Lord. I didn't feel what some of the others felt so sincerely. It was this way with me right through the last night of the children's revival meeting.

I was the only one left who was still unsaved, and the preacher looked at me. He looked at me and announced he would continue the revival, if necessary, for three more nights — just to save

God Lives!